Endlesswill Presents

Broken Perception

EXTENDED VIEWS

Sharon
Thank you
Endlesswill

Writer's Block Publishing
http://www.writersblockpublishing.net/

Broken Perception EXTENDED VIEWS

Copyright 2016 © by William "Endlesswill" Davis Jr.
All rights reserved. Published in the United States of America. First Edition.

Pages 5-33 (25 poems) are available on audio with music accompanying the spoken word. Email *poetendlesswill@gmail.com* for information on how to get your copy.

♫

Pages 5-33 (25 poems) are available on audio
With music accompanying the spoken word
Email **poetendlesswill@gmail.com**
For information on how to get your copy

Table of Contents

Me Short	5	Image	6
Me	7	Poetry	9
Should I Be	10	Friend or Enemy	11
Music	12	Ridicule	13
Words of Wisdom (1)	14	Daddy Song	15
A Moment	16-17	Gave Up	18-19
Parents (1)	20	Parents (2)	21
Words of Wisdom (2)	22	Reflection	23
Island	24	Man's Mind	25
Patience	26	Be Something	27
Jealous	28	Rush	29-30
Running	31	Don't Love Me	32
Thank You	33	Creative	35-36
Different	37	Don't Go To Durham	38-39
Day Dreaming	40	Flower	41
Why	42	Substance Abuse	43
Real Men	44	Anxiety	45
Infected	46	I Miss You	47
Help	48	Have You Ever	49
K'Vian	50-51	Fork in the Road	52
I Hate Thinking Of you	53-54	Drug	55
I Don't	56-57	Haiku Hi	58
Conflict	59	Conversation With Christ	60-61
Picture	62	A Letter to my Eyes	63-64
Affection	65	Angels	67
Apologetic	68-69	Working Man	70
8/14/2014	71-74	Band Aids	75-76
Haiku Music	77	Because it Seems	78-81
Canvas	82	Change Gonna Come	83-84
Cloud 9	85	Free	86
Haiku Running	87	Creative	88
I Am This	89-90	If	91-92
Lie	93	Men Don't Cry	95
Content Capitalism	96	Ghost	97-98
Now	99	Officer Davis	100
Preach	101-104	Save Me	106
Smile	107	Edge of the Bed and Love	108
Super Hero	109-110	Tired	111-112
Bruce Jenner	113	Too Much	114
Twenty-Eight	115	Heartless	116
A Dream	117	[Wrong] Love	118
Memory	119-120	Relationship View	121-122
Tomorrow	123	Words of Wisdom (3)	124
Proof	125	#Writeheavy	128-131

Me - Short

I have great qualities
With a particular personality
Some say I am mean
Others swear by my loyalty
To me
My character is based
On the reflection I see
And the footsteps in front of me
That have shown me ways to succeed
While taking care of my tree
Of
Making me complete
While at the same time focusing on
Being the best Will
I can be

Image

I envision
To create an image that will replenish a real man's image
Something permanent that can never be finished
Just passed on
I refuse to think that I'm the last one with the imagination better
yet motivation to stop waiting and just do
See my passion is so persistent
That life is exquisite
And my mindset will live on through existence
While not caring what the next think praying that the envious
mentality will soon be extinct
Because truly it has no purpose
People not looking at the next because we know what self-worth
Is and hate is nonexistent because that Thought is so worthless
I just need help
Please reach for the positive in you and pass it on because
I can't do it by myself

Me

There is more to me than what you see
A man standing just a little shy of 6 feet
With size 11 1/2 feet
And is here reciting poetry
I am a man that's deep
Deeper than ever ocean and sea
And can relate to its ways
Because no one really knows how deep
I am my own mystery
Product of my past miseries
My present victories
And is so looking forward for what's next for me
In this athletic slender frame
I have so much to gain
And for those of you who think you know me
Because you know my name
I am an endless beach
And what you know is just a simple grain
I look at life with so much to gain
Born as mere lump of clay
And was molded into this
By life's everyday maze
And endless obstacles
My way of thinking is illogical
Compared to the norm
While being so thankful that this is the way I was born
And refuse to conform
In his sticky honeycomb of life
I've strayed away from the swarm
To start my own hive
I can't relate to
"Started from the bottom now I'm here"
Because I have no here
There is no cap to my there
My definition of success and an abyss
Can be compared
My euphoria is endless
Strive relentless
Even as a little cum shot from my dad's spot
I promised myself to be committed
And me being here today
Proves that I did it

My journey will never be finished
I am a story without an ending
Because I have planted my seeds
And I care for them
Watering them with wisdom
And giving them more than everything that they need
They are my reason why I can only succeed
You see
There is more to me than what you see
Behind this frame
Stands a lot of glory and shame
But I realize that through all my worries
That I only have me to blame
Meaning that it up to me to change
So I do it
And for those of you who want to try and criticize
And scrutinize
Keep it to yourself
Because your opinion of me is useless
Literally so unavailing
Because I feel that me worrying about what others think
Would result in steps towards me failing
So instead I stay sailing
On a boat driven by Will
Defined in the Webster's dictionary as:
Intend, desire, drive, want
So again driven by will
So with that as my name
How can I fail

Poetry

Poetry to me
Is a release for the emotions that are deep
I hold my breath and let my pen breathe
Close my eyes and let the words see
It is my art
My poems are the blood pumping through my heart
They are expressions
My confessions
My protection
My weapon to help me control my aggression
For tranquility
Poetry unleashes the will in me
Helps me be me
It is a smooth breeze over a calm sea
It is my Reggie Miller at the garden taunting Spike Lee hitting
Threes
My Stevie wonder making magic over piano keys
Poetry is a baby's first words
The woman in my dream's perfect curves
It is love
It is that high without needing a drug
Its that conversation with Granny followed by a hug
My release
My peace
Just a piece of a way teach those that can be reached
With a way to discuss
When I write I get a rush
And when I recite I feel touched
By a feeling of not being able to get enough
Of this moment in my life
So I write
I am a poet

Should I Be

Should I be what you want me be
As I open my eyes I sometimes wish that I could see what you
see
But only to make it even you've got to share my grief
You can tell me how to live my life if you agree to feel my past
pains piece by piece
And you will realize my passive emotions is just me reaching for
peace
While searching for a release
For the anger that's underneath.
So I just breath
Wishing the acceptance and affirmation
Of the world would just leave
Then I remember to be thankful
And just appreciate being me

Friend or an Enemy

What's worse
A friend or an enemy
I say a friend because most of the time you can't see through
who they pretend to be
I'm not implying that a friendship
Revolves around negativity
But if you're a friend to me
You're really more considered family
This means
We will be that until the end
I have noticed that a friend's loyalty
Often comes with stipulations
And has a tendency
To thrive on jealousy
With the mindset
Of
"What can you do for me"
Instead of
"How may I help you"
Family is there for the problems
To make sure that you see them through
Making sure you are pushing yourself to be a better you
So to all my friends who have become my family
I would like to say thank you.
And I appreciate you
And for you being in my life
I am truly grateful
To all my enemies a part of me wants to hate you
But then I realize that if you think about me enough
To be hateful
Then it's obvious they there is part of me that makes you
And since I am child of God
I've learned to love snakes too

Music

If music is art and rap is music
But everyone is a rapper
Are there any real artists
Or maybe I just can't understand the context
My conscience a little too complex
For lyrics that really lack content
Compressed with a bunch of rhyming words
About selling birds
Smoking herb
Women with curves
Manly self, self, self
Music is meant to have a message not lusting for wealth
The true purpose is to help
Not hate
Which is remanence of hell
Or selling yourself for records to sell
It is Art
Something orchestrated originating at the heart
With feeling
Not guns
Drugs
Or thugs
Things that promote killing
I'm willing to challenge all artists to be far from average
Look inside yourself and un-shelve true talent
Be different
More significant
Make a difference with the music
Because as of lately it has been useless
And the radio tends to prove it
Now I'm not saying to artists that this applies to all
But the category of marvelous music seems to be very small
And I know that I want to hear it
A constant consistency of lyrics
More music that tells stories not telling are kids what beer is
Teaching boys to be men
And being a thug and gangster is the definition of of what fear is
So to all artists I ask that you take a chance to inspire
And not be someone that's looked down upon
But
Someone that's admired

Ridicule

Am I a fool because I ignore the ridicule
Mocked by others because I use my tool
Did I break the rules
Or just break the chain
Demanded change
With an overdeveloped brain
Consider lame because my mindset isn't the same
And I prefer to use the word
Isn't
Instead of
Ain't
So I embrace the hate
And refuse to wait
Realize that I don't need to hear it from you
Because I tell myself I'm great
And I believe it
Keep your sympathy because honestly I don't need it
The world's empathy I bleed it
Success I will exceed it
Since I have already surpassed expectation
I was expected to give up
And I would prefer to work hard for my money instead of hustle
for a quick buck
The difference is I acknowledge my importance
Hence
The relevance of my common sense
This complements my courage to try
Which interjects
The answer the question why
I refuse
To be a muse or an example of another who will lose
So my failures are driving my fate to be great
While accepting the world's ridicule

<u>Words of Wisdom</u> (1)

The glory goes to the one with the biggest Jesus piece
While I wake up and pray for a piece of Jesus's peace
Begging Lord
Please smite this beast inside of me
And bring forth the you inside of me
Be my thoughts
So in me
It will be you that thinks
So while I open my mouth
It is more of you that speaks

Daddy Song

I love my daddy
I love my daddy
I love him
Him so much
I love my daddy
So much
So much
So much
I love my daddy
So much

By Janiah Davis

♫

A Moment

One of the mere moments that I hold onto in my life
March 31, 2008 11:53 p. m.
My eyes burned as they refused to blink
And were red as fresh lit coals off of a Michigan winter camp fire
I thank God for this moment
As my cornea was concrete stuck on that sight
Of right
A moment where you're just so thankful of life
Appreciating every person's presence
As we all are in awe at this present
Better than that first Christmas gift that I can remember
My daughter is being born
And to watch that first breath
I swear to you
I feel like it transferred from mine to her chest
Because I so lost my breath
And that moment gave me the mindset
That I will give her anything
Even my last breath
This is my baby
God's creation
And most people don't believe me
And sometimes begin to tease me
But my daughter cried at that moment
Until I looked into her eyes
Because that looked that I gave her
Reassured her that she was safe
And she was mine
I am a father now
I can honestly remember each second
Thinking that this is a moment of perfection
Saying thank you to God for this blessing
And as the nurses and doctors do their job
I simply stare at my me
Counting toes on her feet
And fingers on hand
At that moment I took a stand
Promising myself to retort away from my boyish ways
And make the choices of a man
I must provide
And as she lay on the table

And the nurses and doctors do their jobs
I begin to cry
And I don't mean weep
Like she will do one day
As she is skating outside and scrapes her knee on the concrete
I mean tears of pride
Because I know that I can be there for her
When she needs someone to dry her eyes
I will be there for her
And to tell her of the ways of a boy
How they will do everything to try
So don't believe their lies
I promise myself to always be there for her
I then begin to smile
Because I know I will never leave
Since at 11:53 p.m. that day
God blessed me with a better me
To help me be a better me
I then begin to watch her sleep
My face so close to hers
I can feel the air move through her nose
I say to myself
This must be what being kissed by an angel feels like

Gave Up

My dad gave up
I've seen pictures and heard stories
About when he was ambitious and had goals and actually tried
But somewhere in his life that part of him died
And I have memories that I hold dear to my heart
About when he would take me to work with him
Teaching me to hold a hammer and saying
"Son hit that nail"
And looking me in the eye and saying
"Son try your hardest at what you want
I guarantee you will not fail and never give up your fight"
But as I converse with him now a days
I want to ask why he didn't take his own advice
And it is not right to see a man let alone your dad
So sad waking up every day so mad
A man filled with such anger
I look at him as stranger a man I don't want to meet
Because I am his Junior and I refuse for that to be me
My dad gave up
A man with six kids
Six baby mama's
3 girls
3 boys
2 failed marriages
So many empty voids
At one time he was my hero my leader
And there are times today when I want to tell you
Dad I need you yet I avoid moments when I can see you
And we resemble each other slightly
So I'm afraid that one day I'll be you
Like a broken reflection
Looking at you is seeing all the dreams I've neglected
There are times when I want to ask you why have you accepted
This life of complacency
Of wait and see
Of merely nothing
My dad gave up
And I am his oldest child
By saying that I'm not saying that I'm affected the most
But I'm the one who must smile
When my siblings come to me with the weight of our father
I have to hide my emotions and show that I'm not bothered

And give those words of encouragement
Make silly jokes and love
Until their worries have gone
My dad gave up
And I am a man with kids
Three boys and two precious girls
I couldn't imagine a day without trying to make them better
Because they are my world
My air
And I refuse to give them an opportunity
To utter the words that their dad was not there
Because I am aware of the feelings that can begin to grow when
you know that
Your dad doesn't care
About himself
Let alone anyone else
So I tie shoes
And watch Blues Clues
And kiss boo boos
And I enjoy it
Because to me
Being a dad is great stuff
And I promise myself and my children that they will never say
My dad gave up

Parents (1)

We are parents
It is apparent
That we hold lives in our hands that should be cherished
Flourished
And protected
Loved
Never misdirected
Allowing them to mess up
Then teaching them to correct it
Learning to never ever give up
And look up
To goals
We are the ones who should unfold
Mold
And hold
And love
As parents we hug
And watch
Ensure that our child's ball is fumbled
But never drops
We teach them to never stop
We are to never stop loving
Treating our kids as gifts
We are their number one fans
We are to hold their hands
Telling them that anything that
They want to be
That we believe that they can
We are their leaders
Their first friends
Mentors
Guides
Helping them to open their eyes
It is a gift to be a parent
Are responsibility as parents
Is to forever strive to be better parents

Parents (2)

I am a creator a molder an architect
Or maybe more even considered a gardener
Because I have planted seeds and I water them with wisdom
Giving them more than everything that they need
They literally control my heartbeat I look at them as they sleep
And that sight reminds me that God has truly blessed me
Without them I was a wandering sheep an incomplete puzzle
Lucky enough to find my missing piece in these
I was a rusted gear and their love has been my grease
Know I'm a well-oiled machine
Just ready for them each day I do this for them
I am a friend but more of a father in the end
Ready to discipline but more to compliment hold hands and love
In my life there has been nothing better to what can compare
To absolutely 100% knowing with all of my being
That for me to walk in my baby's rooms and be able
To watch my little angels begin to start dreaming
My soul starts leaping for joy as I enjoy each moment
And cherish my responsibilities of being a parent I love it
And just can't even begin to comprehend how others don't
Love it
I am no baller or a shot caller
I am a man that plays toys with his little boys and paints the
nails of his daughters
Each day and every day I am there
And when I try to even think about not being in their lives
I get scared because I have seen and been there
Affected by the lack thereof my parents being there
So again each day I'll be there and not only will I be there
But I will take care nurture, respect, protect, love and provide
Because I adore and cherish being able to be in my babies' lives
Nothing in this world will keep me away from them
With broken legs and a bad back
I'm 100% confident that I would stand by their side
Give them piggy back rides
Cook dinner and still have enough energy to
Read a story at night
Put them in their beds and tuck them in tight
They power my pride my kids
Jordan, Janiah, Josiah, Madeleine and Jaiden
My kids are my life
I thank God every day for them being in my life

♫

<u>Words of Wisdom</u> (2)

Our appearance is just a blemish
When I look at your face I see GOD
Because we are all created in his image
So next time you look at your reflection
Enjoy the blessing
Show a little appreciation and smile
God will smile back

Reflection

I only tell my deepest confessions
Mainly to my reflection
I've told him
That I sometimes struggle
With holding the weight of my complexion
Because it's statistically proven that
I'm damn near destined to be in a facility for corrections
So I try my best to control my aggression
In situations where I'm upset
I just take a deep breath and deem it as a lesson
Because anger can grow like an infection
Spreading all over your soul
Leading towards depression
Then you will be mad at the world
In much need of affection
Blinded by your bitterness
Oblivious to your blessings
Living life hit or miss in much need of some directing
But you push away the obvious
Positive things you seem to be rejecting
While you're nearing towards
Negative schemes that's disrespecting
Any and everything
Your reflection is suggesting
And now you realize
You reality is getting messy
So it's back to the mirror
For much more confessing

Island

I've heard profound phrases
Like
Product of my environment
And then I wonder
I live in America
Why does it feel more like an island
Where sad sounds surround us
Like gunshots
Kids crying
And police sirens
Followed by a deathly deep silence
And the world's unaware
Apprehensive to the violence
And most of us can't swim
So we are stuck on this island
In fear of our future
Cause its water all around us
So perturbed at our past
We let the pressure drown us
Without even fighting to swim
So quick to make excuses
That we don't even realize we can change the life that we live
Unsatisfied by our situations and the circumstances we're in
Desperate for desire
But our dreams are buried within our souls
And when you're stuck on an island
How can you strive for goals
With failure as the sand and you're buried as deep as your toes
And the waves are crashing down as memories of bad decisions
you chose
But that's just the life on an island

Man's Mind

The man's mind is tainted mentality manipulated
Originality out the window everything gets duplicated
Controversy debated
I hate it
I suffer from personality displacement
Because I feel as if I'm on the top floor and the world is my
basement
Or I'm walking in the dark and the world is my pavement
But I still feel so much pain
My brain is a slave ship
Heart federal agent
Intelligent conversations
Let's converse quietly
Some thought exchanging
Take a look at my life
And my reality deprivation
My dreams
Slight sensations
Patient
Never slight complacent.
For hatred I'm a racist
If skin is a color
Couldn't we erase it
But it's permanent
Life can be dirty
We're just the worms in it
With the choice to choose our own flaws
Do you know what is your poison is

Patience

Patience
Is the sensation
That is key for greatness
However
My generation generates so much hatred
That the expectations
For the nation are deteriorating
I'm explaining the outlook of the world that's hating on the
beautiful
Colors of mother nature's paintings
Our hatred never hesitating
Now I'm questioning
Who should we be blaming
You
Me
Let's just say TV
Or
Let's point fingers at the government for making us all crazy
It seems like we're loving it
The material slavery
I'm a victim of it too
One of many so blame me
It may be
The pain we're sustaining
No one has the answers
But everyone's complaining

Be Something

Set a goal and achieve it
Say you are somebody important and believe it
What do you see as your tomorrow
Look more at simply where you stand
Prepare positive footprints for you to follow
Know you are great and do more than what it takes
When life seems to have you on a chase embrace the race
Run 'til you are tired, until your feet are crying
Legs dying, lungs burning
Literally yearning for a break
Then run some more until you lap life
Enjoy victory because each day you wake up
Be proud because your past pains are now history
So breathe that breath and realize that you are in your "first place"
So keep going and start believing or more so knowing that you are a gift, a rarity, a vital piece in someone's peace
So important relatable to air so be there
Whether it's a friend, a family member, a child
Maybe even your child
Realize that someone
Whether you realize someone looks at you for care
So when the next opportunity is there for you to face your reflection
Look it in the eyes and begin the stare
Stand with pride
Let it know that you are not scared and for anything that's in your way
That it better beware because you are aware
Of the person you see and the immensity that is there
Tell yourself you're amazing stand tall in amazement
Then bask in your greatness and focus
Be proud that your potential is the ocean
Deep uncharted territory your desires are your Destiny
With fate being the author of your story
The acknowledgements in the end mirror the accomplishments
Achievements and moments when you have succeeded
Hence exceeded the world's stereotypes
You are original no other like, unique, extraordinary
Compared to you all others all things are nothing
But these words are nothing
Unless you realize that you can be something

Jealous

I am jealous
Jealous of your clothes
Envious of your bed sheets and the moments that they hold
I wish I could hold you that way
Protecting your dreams covering you as you lay
I can be your pillow mold me to your comfort
Pushing your hands against me massaging me to your liking
Then rest your head on me and I'll caress your thoughts
Helping you relax as you enjoy comfort
On your cloud 9 of myself
Soothing your body
Your soul melts
Meshes
Confesses to me
As you rest
You are a blessing to me
Your comfort compressing
Calm feelings of ease
As you are smothered by me
Your lover as your comforter
The essence of serenity seep into the air
Keeping us high from the pheromones
Perspiring from our bodies
Inhaling this heaven
Exhaling our confession
Of expressing
This loving
Being the recipe
Of you and me
Mixed with forever
Love
Compassion
Together
Stirred with the utensil of affection
Mixed in a bowl of perfection
We prepare our meal of a perfect match
Feeding one another pieces of ourselves
Savoring each bite
You melting on my tongue
The explosion of your flavor
Dance on my taste buds
You are my delight

Rush

She looked back at me as if she has been crushed
When I looked deeply into her eyes
And say that I don't want to rush
Followed by me stating
That I don't want to start to open your heart
Off the inadequacies of lust
So as much as it is killing me
I have promised myself to refuse to touch
Until you have given me your trust
Which to me is the most important part of yourself
I want to know about when you were a child
And where did you get your smile
What are things that bother you
That make you want to frown
I want you to know so that I don't want to push those buttons
So instead of just fucking
We sat up
Relaxed and conversed for hours
Literally just lost in the time
Feeling that attraction of intimacy
As we simply share our minds
Clothes on
But thoughts naked
On edge with anticipation
Of that next word
Admittedly so ready just off the sexy curves
Of only your lips
How they contort with when you get serious
And your facial expression shows that much more emphasis
As I wait for the break while we converse
To give you a soft kiss
Then you whisper to me that you can no longer resist
Followed by
"How much longer do we have to wait"
Giving me that look that reassures me you want me to penetrate
Because between your legs have begun to saturate
Your sensitivities salivate
As you anticipate each breath I take
Awaiting that move I make
Towards your frame
Then I hesitate

And you can no longer contain
So she looks at me and says
"Come over here babe"
Then slowly kisses on my neck
(And who doesn't like that)
Then pulls down my shorts and gives it kiss
Yes gives it a kiss
And begins to taste
That part of myself
That I'm so proud of below my waist
My heart starts to race
Blood pumping through my veins
(And I bet she could tell)
Because her hands are wrapped around me
As I begin to swell
Literally growing in front of her eyes
Then this lovely lays on my bed
Pulls down her pants
And opens her thighs
And fuck all that bullshit
I'm not going to lie
I looked at the perfection with that
Already swimming pool wetness
So I had to dive in
Trying to drown myself
Because who needs to breathe
Mindset Thanksgiving dinner
Don't really care how much I eat
And she begins to rub on my back as she watches me feast
While saying sexy things to me like
I'm the man of her dreams
And
Put me inside her
I then give those lower lips one last kiss
And then begin to lay down beside her
Lifting her legs and starting with the tip
She then grabs on my hand and starts to nibble it
We enjoy each other all day
Enjoying being tired in that right way
So shocked and intrigued at the passion
And this was only our first date
......to be continued.......

Running

♫

My mind's running
And I've accepted the fact
That it will never stop
It has to keep running from the things I forgot
While I hope not to forget
That half of the things that I will be forgiven for
I haven't even done yet
So should I have regret
But living in regret will only suppress the man I haven't become yet
So as I'm running
I'm wondering
What will happen if I don't run
If I stop
Will that ultimately mean that I have won
Or
Will the thoughts start winning
And have me remembering
Why I was even running from the beginning
So I'm lost
Or have I just lost
So I've accepted the answer
That I'm just running from my past
Thoughts

Don't Love Me

So you love me and trust me and want to be with me
You say I make your life complete
Well I'm sorry but I've heard that before
I have often even enjoyed that song and sang to its tune
Myself have been wooed
Into thinking that one can be made from two
Now I stand here my heart just used as a tool to keep me alive
Because to my surprise all of my past tries
Left me looking like a fool for Love
So yes I have given up
I'm sick of trying
Unknowingly internally dying and poisoned by words
Mere glimpses of good feelings
I've even been caught kneeling
Confessing the secrets of my heart
Looking that one that was supposed to be that one
In the eye
My pride set aside
Flooded with the facade of love being alive
She was supposed to my bride
And I am aware that is unfair to compare
You at this moment being the apple of my eye
To my past pear
However that justifies love being lie
And I know that some of you while you listen
Maybe thinking my thoughts are restricted
And I have just been a victim of a broken heart
But how many times have you given love a try
Think about it
Times when you had love in your life and it died
Simple faded into a memory so when I hear the words
"I love you"
It just offends me
Because I am certain your feelings are just pretending
So I am doing my part in preventing the possibility
Or the certainty of me hurting you or you hurting me
Don't love me
Because I'm sure you don't even know how to do it
Your words are just useless
And every one of your past relationships where you were
"In love"
Proves it

Thank You

♫

Is it even possible
I know it's seem logical
But I wonder if it's an impossible obstacle
To actually give thanks
Show how much you really appreciate
The fact that God woke you up this day
To simply say thanks
Can't be enough
The magnitude of my gratitude
Can't even be compared to the measure
Of the world's longitude and latitude
If needed I'd walk the distance from the earth to the moon
Which has been charted at 238,857 miles
To express with every breath in my chest
That God gives me reasons to smile
That he has given me the opportunity to be here now
So I stand proud
The simple two word sentence of
"Thank"
And
"You"
In conjunction honestly is so redundant
Considering his ability to wake up everyone in the world
And still remember me
While giving me the eyes to see
And giving me the mouth to speak
And ability to reach underneath the man inside of me
To bring forth the ways he gave me
He keeps giving
Just giving
And I'm taking
While wanting
And he is giving
And I'm taking
And all I seem to say
All He ever wants me to say
Is thanks

Creative

I can only be creative
My melanin surface is my soil
My entirety is Earth
There is
So
Much more
Implanted
Within this Will
Thoughts watered with will
Driven
Foot full-force to the pedal
As I pick the poems
From the rose
Of concrete growth
Chanting
Success loves me
Success loves me not
Success loves me
Success loves me not
A game of Russian roulette
Played with foresight of dreams
Not yet met
So I plant
Plans
Proceeding
To break ground
A seed
To life
And I
Can see
The
Light
Born blind
But by my stride
Has given me foresight
So again I grow
Weather comes
But I grow
And think about it
A plant survives off of the sunlight
And it also lives through the night
That next day
When you see it

It's different
It's stronger
More vibrant
It doesn't worry
So why worry
Is that rhetorical question
That's repeated
So I can remember
That my
Roots have spread
Strengthening thought
Making room for growth
And when flower sees the sun
When I see the sun
And my being
Puts connection to source
Plays math
With me
And the day
Equaling a positive
By the square root of a sun ray
It does something
This feeling you can't really name
As if newborn crying to light of first sight
And when it feels its mother
When baby presses touch to heart
It stops crying
It's calm now
The warmth of the sun
Compared to a mother
Holding life
Soothing sorrow
For a new day that has begun
It's appreciated
Enjoyed
And soothed
Now I
Have managed to put that passion
To a plan
Now I'm just waiting
Watching progress grow

Different

It's been said before
That history repeats itself
Meaning something done
Will be done again
So is anything ever done
Is there really one
Original thought
If the apple doesn't fall too far from the tree
Is to make hint that one's life
Living is similar to the one who planted it
Therefore meaning the seed
Subsequently
Grew from cement
Or is it possible for roots to branch
Form veins in prior stains
That help strengthen a path for change
So someone
Anyone
Sometimes I think
Maybe even me
Can be
Different

Don't Go to Durham

"Don't go to Durham"
Is what I heard that first day I stepped foot into this Triangle
The Triangle is what they call it
As my self-proclaimed tour guide of the city told me
Cary is the nice part
Raleigh is the nice part
But
"Don't go to Durham"
Is what I heard
As if the Triangle was scalene
And Durham was on the short end
Standoffish to the nice parts but there nonetheless to complete the Triangle
And from Grand Rapids, Michigan
To Raleigh, North Carolina being my transition
In Michigan played victim to many environmental "bad parts"
So this man with new self-proclaimed change of heart
Didn't go to Durham
Stayed in the area that was "safer"
According to the man giving me a lesson
Or lack thereof
Of my new surrounding
Portrayed Durham as a city drowning
And if you didn't want to swim too deep
Then you should avoid Durham's waves
Is what I heard
Like I was being warned of danger
And the depths of Durham being too deep for new travelers
But one can only swim waist high for so long
And diving head-first is always more entertaining than shallow waters
So I dive
Feeling like I am breathing underwater
As I see and learn
About
History
Close eyes and retract
Historic events when people wanted to come to Durham
Fought for rights in Durham
I read about
Fights for segregation
And 29-year-old Reverend Douglas Moore
Getting arrested amongst others from Durham

For sitting at the wrong side of an ice cream parlor
And ignoring the ignorance of the assigned seating
White side and black side
Don't go to Durham
Is what I heard
As if I was being warned from the dangers
Of...of...
I still don't know
In a city where proud people stood up for their rights
And stood ground for their city
Were arrested for merely color of complexion
In a time where equality was fought for
And stood ground on the minor luxurious like
A vanilla waffle cone ice cream
On one of those hot Durham days
Don't go to Durham
Why I question
When Durham at one time was in recognition for its progression
I read about the article written in 1912 by W. E. B. Du Bois
Titled
The Up-building of Black Durham:
The Success of the Negroes and Their Value to a Tolerant and
Helpful Southern City
The title alone gave me the chills
As it introduced pride
And the want to try to change a distorted view
For a better and more relevant
Durham
So I began to swim more
Diving deeper into history
Back stroking into moments in time
Learning of communities
Black-owned business
Jobs
Factories
Unity
102 years later
It is up to you and me
Not only for Durham
But each side of the Triangle should all be viewed congruently
Equal
So I say come to Durham
Because Durham definitely has some things it can teach you

Haiku
Day Dreaming

Eyes closed daydreaming
Sounds of laughter around bliss
Applause winning....... Thanks

Flower

I wonder if a flower ever looks at the sun
At that moment only twice a day when the sun touches the earth
And gives birth
Plants life unto our life
I really wonder does a flower
Ever say
Thank you
Does it appreciate the reach from the sun's rays
Or does it just exist
Not knowing the sun's work to let life breathe
The reach of its heat
Does a flower
Ever say
Thank you
There are moments in life
Where that appreciation is needed
Someone or something looked at me
Someone looked at you and put arms out
And rays of ways
Were reaching out leading for better
There is something so amazing about the sun
Lack of its heat has been linked
To lack of Vitamin D
Subsequently leading towards depression
The acronym for the state of mind is called S. A. D.
Seasonal Affective Disorder
Being affected
To the point where anger is reflected
One's being is infested
Lack of control with no hold
All conscious is compressed in
It's really sad
There is something so amazing about the sun
It rises and sets twice a day
With the unpredictability of a cloud
There is no telling if it will shine your way
So some seem to seldom sun chase
Running towards unpredictable
Instead of realizing one's own
Twice a day
Look at your help
And showing that you appreciate

Why

Why should we try when the passion has died
Is it to fill up our hearts with hope only to lead to further demise
Or only for more lies to arise ending in more cries
This is followed by the unanswerable question haunting our
Minds
Why
Why must we give our all while only accepting half
Why must we love so hard only to be let down so easily
Why do we get it right
Then destroy that right with yet another fight
Why I must ask
Do we hide the feelings that made us laugh
And then run away from yet another perfect day
With the one that we want to take our breath away
Why is it so hard to forgive the ones we love
When they make that unexplainable mistake
Why do we stick around only to be let down with more heartache
Why love so hard that we spend nights
Where we are supposed to hold each other while we sleep
Frustrated so we just lay awake
Thinking of the many moments that seemed driven by fate
Where our relationship was an example of something truly great
Now as I look at your face you give me expressions of disgrace
And all I'm left to say is I'm sorry
I'm sorry for the deceit and for being weak
I'm sorry for every tear you've shed and the thoughts that you
are left to think but please know that I see and I realize that you
are precious and unique a rare pearl have faith in
Believing that you are my world and I want this forever
We have the strength to conquer any endeavor
But we just need to complement one another so we can do it
together
And promise to never let it weaken
With love it's strengthened and stays strong to hold on
So why should we give up I haven't had enough
No more times that's tough or thoughts of discuss
It's obvious our love hasn't died we've just got to try
As we are looking ahead kind words being said
No more why only accept never regret or negativity
Because there have been too many moments
That proves that you complete me
I'm sorry

Substance Abuse

Sad to admit that I have often overdosed
However I am not ashamed
So numb from the feel of dumb
That I don't feel shame
I'm too distracted
From the thrill of adrenaline
Moving through my veins
While relaxation and a rush
Play tag in my brain
Feeling high and then low
Heart racing
While moving slow
Addicted
To my medication
Overindulging in my pain killers
Abusing my prescription
When I want it
I feel conflicted
Thoughts restricted
Sight tunnel-vision
Damn near can't function
Without this substance
Hating
While loving
This substance abuse
Of
You

Real Men

I sometimes try and figure
What is really a "real nigga"
Not saying that I'm something bigger or even different
But to consider myself a nigga just sounds so ignorant
And I'm very much significant
With a mindset that's magnificent
So I simply acknowledge the fact that I'm something better
So I ask
Is it necessary to add an "A" in place of the known "E-R"
To describe the "real" person that we are?
Especially us with kids
What are we really telling them
By referring to ourselves as
"Real niggas"
Just because our skin has melanin
And that just sounds crazy
I will not refer to myself as a real anything that is used as a
term by racists
And that has similarities to a word used for hatred
So instead of
"Real niggas"
I will call us
"Real greatness"
And I will say it with my head held high
And if I hear someone call themselves a
"Real nigga"
I'll make sure to stop and ask them why
Because to me it has no meaning
And is more of something demeaning
So I will say that enough is enough
Because every time I hear "real nigga" I just stand in disgust
And I question what the term reflects
Disrespect
Reject
Neglect
And the lack thereof intellect
So I ask all my brothers to take a stand
When you look in the mirror don't see a "real nigga"
Because you are definitely

"Real Men"

Anxiety

Is it pure anxiety
Or is it realizing I'm not the person I've been trying to be
Life is frightening
Cause I'm trying to stay focused while I'm steady fighting
Demons deep inside of me
If my thoughts were a painting the canvas would be a sight to
See
Genius I might be almost enlightening
Yet ignorant to brilliance and the significance to doing the right
Thing
But is it relevant
More so than less
Cause I still question my intelligence and my circumstance
Why does life hurt so much when they say that life's
Heaven-sent
I say life's a bitch
But I blame myself because life is what you make of it
I need a break from it
To take a look at my life and all the mistakes that I've made in it
Success is what I aim to hit
And my potential is presidential
My mental is just maintaining it

Infected

I have been affected
No, infected by this sickness
Of falling victim to lies of life
A fiend for fantasy
Injecting fairy tale into my veins and enjoying that high
Smiling while I ride that cloud 9 of never
A bird without feathers
Looking over the ledge
Seeing other's soar
Knowing that for me that there must be more
So I look up
Spread my wings and jump
Wind against my body enjoying my try
At the attempt to fly
Then as I open my eyes
I fall to the floor
Love being my blood
Leaking from my pores
Pride and emotions left sore
So how could I not be
Hesitant
Or more so
Apprehensive to attempt to fly for your
Love

I miss you

I miss you
But how can I miss something I never had
You are my fast break looking at that goal
Running
Ready to dunk but I get an overthrown pass
A piece missing in my past
Should have been my moment
You are my moment
Maybe subconsciously
You are the reason I am a poet
A memory that is slightly faint
However my mind refuses to let go of it
Keeping it locked away
Protected
As a tool
For us to maybe grow with
I am so ready for our first kiss
Anticipating being with you
So you are no longer missed
So for me it's frustrating that I have to settle for this
I miss you

Help

I often tell myself
Fuck help
You can do it all by yourself
I am all that I need
I look in the mirror and yell
"All you need is me"
You are the only apple on the world's last tree
The loan shark swimming in the sea
A mere recluse
I often need others but I think
"What's the use"
You are alone
Your mind is your home
Nobody to call because no one would answer the phone
A man without a friend
A book without an end
A walk by yourself longing for a friendly hand
But yet you still manage to stand
So be proud
You're so ahead of the crowd
But if pride is what I have then why do I still manage to frown
Living through the tears of a clown
The lion who is feared
Yet no one hears him growl
Screaming at the top of my lungs
But I can't hear a sound
The beast that is afraid of the mouse
Thus I'm left to accept
That I am by myself until I ask for help

Have you ever....

Have you ever been in love
Must be one of the saddest questions that can be asked
I say this because that question
Implies that love once was in your grasp and it slipped
Simply fell from your grip
And like an old lady with a bad hip you no longer stand the same
And begin to question if you were to blame
And if there were things that you should have changed
As you feel the pain of your heart strain
You remember that
You miss it
You miss that place
That face
And you say to yourself that relationships are like
Marathons
Not a race
So why didn't we pace
Both treated love as a game
Played one another like a stage
Just a level of love to conquer and not look back
However, we said that we loved one another
And reassured that we meant that
By telling each other yours was mine and mine was yours
Then as we break up and reverse those words of love
We separated yours from mine
And mine from yours
This then reassures me that it wasn't love
Because love endures
More than feeling
Almost considered a concept
Endless
Forever
Eternity
Two people pasted
Glued together by a word
A gift that each person is willing
To cherish and protect
A gift that is given each day
Opened up with open arms
So have I ever been in love
At one time I thought so
But since the love is no longer with me
I honestly can say that I'm not sure

K'Vian

Mom, can you help me out of bed
Mom, can you help me get dressed
Mom, can you help me use the bathroom
Mom
Mom
Mom
Can you
Can you
Can you
Is what echoes throughout the walls of this home
And to the blind eye this may seem like a needy child
But no he just can't do it on his own
You see my friend K'Vian is 16
6'3" but was born with muscular dystrophy
And for those of you who don't know what that means let me
Educate you
Muscular Dystrophy is labeled as a group of muscle diseases
That weaken the musculoskeletal system and hampers
Locomotion
It is characterized by progressive skeletal muscle weakness
Defects in muscle proteins and the death of muscle cells and
Tissues
So at the age of 16 he seems weak
Pieces of him are dying inside of him so it is hard for him to
Stand on his own feet
And the first thing he says to me when we meet is
"Do I want play one-on-one?"
So I repeat he seems weak
But he asks with such confidence like he just knew he would win
Like Kobe Bryant playing a 12-year-old kid almost arrogant-like
That first impression let me know this would be a kid I would like
We sat and talked for hours about the stuff that we liked
And then laughed at the fact that we both like to write
And the whole time I'm thinking I can't help but to admire his
Fight
Because despite that his muscles cells are water to a sand hill
Slowly but constantly chipping away
Every day he smiles and refuses not to enjoy life
He is an everyday reminder that for me to ever be angry is not
Right
Then I stand in shock when he says that he looks up to me
But yet I admire him so it seems like we are living vicariously
I have even at one time envied his disease

Envisioned myself growing up with muscular dystrophy
And the difference my life would be
To have his food on my plate I even imagine the taste
Then he says to me so casually that today was a good day
This is a moment in my life
Where I realize my worries are a waste
Because here is this child who barely has feeling below the waist
Yet he wakes up daily with a smile on his face
K'Vian is one of my many friends that I truly appreciate
Because that 16 year old kid showed me true humbleness and is
the essence of grace

I've been praying everyday
that I will make it through this pain
So each day that I wake up
makes me appreciate my yesterday

Thank you K'Vian

Fork in the Road

I am at a fork in the road
And it's time to choose a direction
So I question
Stop and wait
Ponder
And begin to start guessing
Which way to go
Who knows
Is it you
Should I take your advice and simply do what you say do
But if I do
Am I being me
Should I worry about defeat
If I choose the wrong path
What would the world think
Or are those thoughts of a mind that's weak
Why am I so scared that my feet seem stuck in the concrete
So I wait
Then I begin my internal debate
The left way or the right way
Which one is my fate
So I choose
While at the same time struggling with the possibility of this
being the path where I lose
And I'm haunted
Maybe this isn't the choice that I really wanted
So I hesitate
And once again I begin to wait
As I struggle with a decision
Choices being restricted
Afraid of clinging onto commitment
Scared of which choice is the right one
Being so indecisive
Not knowing an angle to approach
So
I'm left to be distracted by this fork in the road

I Hate Thinking of You

I hate that I still think of you
And that those thoughts make me think of love dying
Memories of a murder that I was a part of
Damn near a reenactment of that movie *Saw*
As we played games with our feelings
Trapping them in torture chambers of harsh words
And unattainable goals
We even took turns being Jigsaw
Making myself an accomplice to heartache
Literally living an obvious lie
Waking up every day telling myself that the love was real
When deep down I knew it was fake
I was convinced by the deception that us meeting was fate
But it is apparent that we should have looked the other way
Our emotions were mere illusions
Compared to image we really portrayed
Had one another convinced that we were a priceless portrait
Something permanent
But the image slowly began to fade until it was completely
Erased
A moment that was bittersweet and in the beginning was hard to
swallow
Now I have gotten accustomed to the taste
An end to the facade of forever being my food for thought
Left with no choice other than to devour the plate
So full from the failure of what we tried to accomplish
That I have yet to hunger for another
Some have even asked if I'm on a diet
As they try and pick meals for me suggesting I try it
But considering my glutton for you in the past I have to deny it
While hunger pains keep me up at night tempting me
My focus helps me fight because I have experienced first hand
That not everything that smells good tastes right
Some meals need to marinate just a little bit longer
Luckily the best thing about a heart is once it is broken and
Battered
It gets stronger built better each time it's weakened
With addition to the mind now added to the commitment
Your whole person can now proceed to start thinking
Of things your relationship lacked
And realizing that I was attracted by your space
Pressured by your gravitational pull
So I couldn't focus on pulling back
And while you were focused on pulling I was loving

But you were pushing away that
This brought forth reasons for us to retract
React with fights and counter attacks
Verbal slaps resulting in us obviously falling off track
I hate the fact
That me thinking of you
Reminds me of love not given back

Drug

Drug
I need that
I want that drug
Fiend for
Bleed for
And when I have had it I want more
Of this drug
Yet I question if this is even for me
The feeling
Of high and dreading when it says goodbye
And I'm feeling low as I come down
From the thrill of that damn drug

Love is my drug

I Don't

I don't want to be in love
I don't want you to love me
And I know that it may sound mean
But just listen
Let me finish
I don't want to be in love
I want to live it
I have been in love way too many times
And those memories in my mind bring forth anger that's very
Vivid
I've told those relationships bye
And honestly I don't miss it
I want more for me and you
Because "love" isn't enough
Statistically proven over 50% of all marriages will fail
So facts show that I'm telling the truth
So please don't say you love me
Because I won't say I love you
Let's allow our actions to be the proof
I want our feelings for one another to be tattooed
Permanent
Forever
Without having to mention
Of it being in existence
Just aware of it being there
Can we be an island
Just you and I in sight
As we open our eyelids
And our future is so open
Which is the water the surrounds us
And we will stay afloat
On more than just love and hope
And the façade of good times and sweet things being spoke
When the waves start to crash and attempt to sink our boat
We will work together
And will never
Think about growing apart
I want to be your heart
Each part of me as vital as each artery
I'm a growing tree
And you can be each leaf
Put together we make shelter for the world's beauty
Two making one

We are sky to sun
Rain to cloud
Face to smile
Amazing individually
But combined
Wow
The things we can do
I more than just love you
You are the air I inhale
Boat to my sail
Each day I'm so amazed
I am so sincere of me never loving you
Because that love we have to give
Will soon begin to fade
Treated as a phase
A well-read
Very interesting portion
But we always tend to turn the next page
So let's be a story
Instead of just a particular scene
Let's be the index
Introduction
Conclusion
And all the detail in between
King to Queen
And we treat opinions as if they're jesters
Just there for our amusement
Laughing at their attempts for attention
But in the back of our mind we know they're useless
Realizing that we only need you and I to do this
This living
Love tends to seem so circumstantial
There during happy
But during turmoil so hard to handle
Good to hear
But I fear that with only love there's something missing
So let's never start loving
But instead have our feelings for one another
Be the best part of our living

Haiku
Hi

Hi what is your name
Serenity perfected
Do it again please

Conflict

How can I begin to comprehend this
Simple conflict in our relationship
This lack of trust is the pirate on Satan's ship
Driven through fire we both are liars
So ashamed who's to blame
Can it change when hearts are hurt
Can it work when our feelings are ignored
You call me a dog and I call you a whore
This pain is heart surgery how long can we endure
You yell and say that I am no longer yours
Because you can't fight the sight of another woman caressing
My pores
Which is followed by you crying and slamming the door
As I beat on wall while pictures fall on the floor
Glass is shattered
Thoughts are scattered and so are feelings
Is there a healing
Some say yes
But we both question if we are able to accept
The weight of us choosing neglect
Along with the depth of regret
So this is it
The lack of commitment will be our deficit
All our love irrelevant and anger will now take precedence
Broken over mistakes
Love just thrown away
Because it's so much easier to escape
Than to look at each other's faces
So we chose to run away
Avoiding confronting choices we made
While questioning if we are only cheating ourselves
By simply skipping to the next page
When the story was getting so good but instead of fighting it out
We leave because we could
And most said we should
Then there are times when you wish that we would
Have tried again
Remembering great times in the relationship
But then reality sets in
That putting our conflicts over our compassions
Is what really made us end
So the only thing left to say then is
Goodbye

Conversation with Christ

If I had a conversation with Christ
About many topics
One of which being life
Not my life or any one person's particular life
Just life in general and Christ's purpose on all
People's lives
I'm curious of what he would say to me
Would he begin by quoting John 3:16

> "For God so loved the world, that
> He gave his only begotten Son,
> That whosoever believes in him
> Should not perish, but have
> Everlasting LIFE"

I then imagine myself crying while trying to confess my sins
being frustrated because of the life that I have lived and being
ashamed because I wouldn't even know where to begin so as
I'm confessing Christ calmly reads Isaiah 64:6

> "We are all infected and impure with sin
> When we display our righteous deeds,
> They are nothing but filthy rags.
> Like autumn leaves,
> We wither and fall
> And our sins sweep us away like the wind."

As he finishes I yell out
"Please Lord, save me from me!
Clean me from this anger
From this weakness
Destroy this heart that's so mean"
While I'm praying Christ reaches out and I drop to my knees.
Then he begins to recite Colossians 1:13

> "For he has rescued us from the dominion
> Of darkness and brought us into the kingdom
> Of the Son he loves,
> In whom we have redemption,
> The forgiveness of sins."

Then I ask about my purpose
And in this world full of sin

I can't help but to feel so worthless
Then I beg to the King to please make me His servant
As I begin to reach for his hand
I ask him to take this man out from inside of me
And grow me into the angel I am
Then he looks at me smiling
Reassuring that today is anew
With his head raised high he recites Exodus 23:20-22

*"See, I am sending an angel ahead of you
to guard you along the way and to bring you to the place I have
prepared.
Pay attention to him and listen to what he says.
Do not rebel against him; he will not forgive your rebellion, since
my Name is in him.
If you listen carefully to what he says and do all that I say,
I will be an enemy to your enemies and will oppose those who
oppose you."*

And as he finishes I am frozen
In awe that I
A sinner
Have been chosen
To walk with righteousness on a path that's golden
And I'm left saying thank you
And Lord I will praise you
For giving me opportunity at life
Lord I'm so grateful

Picture

It begins with a photographer
Because your beauty was so new to me
So a picture of you I just had to have
I will probably look at it everyday
Or
Until my eyes have another chance
To be amazed by your face
And that picture is perfection
But it does no justice to your face
It doesn't show how your cheekbones rise to your smile
Like the moon to a long day
Or how your eyes glisten like the stars in the sky
I have often wondered
If the reason the sun hides
Is because it realized
That compared to you
It will never shine as bright
Your beauty is such a wonderful site
So I cling to this image
And when I'm not looking at this picture
I'm thinking of you
And the memory is quite vivid
I barely blink
In fear of not staring at your face might make me forget it
A man conflicted
As I appreciate the photo
My heart moves in slow-mo
Because I am frightened
That with all of the everything that you have
That this picture is all I have to hold onto
You're so beautiful

A Letter to my Eyes

Dear eyes,
I would like to start off by saying
I don't believe you two anymore
At the young age of 28 I realize that you both lie
You've deceived me into believing that what I've seen
What you've seen is what I've got
But that is not true
Mere illusions
Just tricks of deception and I wonder
Question why
Why would you do this
Have me chasing like a greyhound on a track
Running after a facade
Like a dog wanting a play toy
No many play toys
Thinking I would
Or could win what you
My pupils had me chasing
Running full speed heart racing
Anticipating a prize
Racing on what I thought was life's track
But was really a treadmill
Going nowhere fast after a goal that you've seen
Made my mind believe was truth but was really a mirage
My brained drained by fantasy
Again I don't
Won't believe you anymore
And I ask you both
Eyes why
I question
Why choose deception
I remember the first time they begged
For that Thundercat action figure
"*Thundercats Hoooo*"
I loved that cartoon
My sister said it was doll
But I wanted it
They
My eyes made me want it
Fully tricked-out action figure with pull-back snapping arm
Detachable sword
I already had the pajamas
I had to have it
My eyes convinced my brain

That I had to have it
On television
My vision
Thought it could fly
And my eyes were so mesmerized
That my mind was blind to reality
Knew of the lie
But I
My eyes
Made me want it
So I begged and pleaded
Eyes made me feel as if I needed it
Then I had it
It didn't fly
The pull-back was weak
The damn thing lasted a week
I was only 5
Now 23 years later you still lie
How dumb of me to finally see
That what you see is not real
Only fabrication
That fuels aggravation
So you both
I promise you
You're only there for appearance
Don't cry
I don't want to hear it
You have done this to yourself
Making me mislead me
I will no longer follow your lead
I'm sorry
I feel bad
That you both
Are just
Sorry

With much regret,
Endlesswill

Affection

Can I start with a question?
We argue and bicker over something that to the other it is
Nothing
Confrontation makes us disgusted
Is that the meaning of affection
Our limits steadily tested
Equaling heavy aggression
This isn't what we expected
Less communication constitutes our relationship being neglected
And we are aware but we avoid
It's sad to see what we have accepted it
Comfortable with the tension
You're always yelling and fusing
Not to mention the constant bitching
This isn't what I've envisioned
So I'm cancelling my commitment
I must
Because I can't be stuck in a relationship that lacks trust
I won't
And I can say I love you a million times
But deep down I really don't

Angels

We are all born Angels
Burdened by death
With the release of first breath
The toxins of violence
Indifference
And judgement
Infiltrate our lungs
It seems we're safer where we had slept
With eyes wide to the world's prize
Among the first sight of light
All innocence has left

Who's going to save us?

Apologetic

I'm really sure when we ALL die
That the first thing God will do is apologize
God will say sorry for the many shades
And the hues of our different views
This lack of understanding of what he/she created
I'm pretty sure God will say sorry
Confident that he/she will explain color
And let us know that we took it all out of context
Then God will ask
Why were we so scared of color
Why were we so proud of color
He/she will ask
Why did we put so much importance on beauty
He/she will explain to the point that
Imagination implants imagery into explanation
And God with such conviction will tell us simply
That on one rainy heaven day
He/she was feeling creative
So God began a beautiful painting
And we
Our colors was what was created
Letting us know that every unique color used
Made perfection
And from his/her point of view
When he/she
Our God
Looked at that creation
He/she
Didn't see hatred
Discrimination or pride of importance
On different portions of his/her painting
He/she just saw God
Which is us
Meaning you
I'm sure that God will then wave hand
Create a massive rainbow
With the beauty of a newborn innocent soothing
And God will ask us
"Which one of these colors represents your world's hate?"
With no answer to speak
God will then teach
That every one color
Every shade

Every hue
That we view
Is God meaning you
And
He/she will then say
I am so sorry for all the confusion
God will then tell us
That it doesn't even matter now
Because we are in heaven
God will then laugh
Mocking our coined phrase of
"God don't make no mistakes"
And again he/she will apologize
For the black
The white
The yellow
The red
All of the colors
And mainly the un-comfortability of what our eyes seen
And what we decided to worldly point out
And God will explain that we are now one
We have risen above the clouds so smile
Put outer down
Lay to bury the worry and pride of our outside
And God will then open arms wide
Consoling away our much needed loss with a hug
And he/she
Our God
Will let us know that we can
Finally live now

Working Man

I spit a poem to man I worked with on Monday
A man whose hands still bleed
From the work we did on Sunday
And when I was finished with my last line
I looked into his eyes
And he began to cry
I was shocked
Because this poem was not a sad poem
Nor thought provoking
It was about my daughter
And the memories that I have
Of the first time our souls started joining
About when she was born
And her laughter I has holding
A giggle blessed to me by God
And was placed into my palm
The poem is called "Moment"
But at this moment
My memory's moment had a man broken
I must be honest
I usually never stop talking
I think my lungs are well past exhausted
But at this moment words were forgotten
And he asked me
This working man
Why am I working man
Acknowledging my talent of speech
Being able to speak to the point that I can make
A grown man
A working machine operator
230lb 6 foot 3 inches man
Shed tear
He looked up
Eyes circling our surroundings
And he asked
Why am I here

8/14/2014

On August 14, 2014 I met a man
A man that smelled of yesterday's pains
His clothes were stained
With I assumed years of old stains
And he walked like his size 6 foot frame
Couldn't bear the burden of the day
Right foot slightly ahead
Like his left couldn't let go of what he had left
But he smiled
He smiled that amazing
6-year old kid
Flying on the swing smile
When their mind
Plays tag with sky and the earth
They're feet inches away the treetop
While their back is parallel to the dirt
That feeling of adolescent freedom smile
And I wondered why
How
And again why
Why choose this life of peasant and beg
Only fed by those who feel sorry
I felt so sorry
And I wondered how
How did he lose himself
A man lost in his losing
Self-inflicted abusing
And the misusing of *try*
And again
I wondered why
How
And why he still smiled
How he still smiled
Again
Why is he smiling
So I approached him
Hesitantly as if my status
Would break down his stature
And the mix of my smooth oil would
Repel his tainted water
And I said
I'm sorry
Like I put those clothes with size handprint holes on his back
And his reply was why

How
And again why
With that toddler innocent smile gone
Replaced with confusion
And his eyes now enraged with question
And then he began to speak
So deep
With the voice of James Earl Jones speaking as Mufasa on his
Peak
He was serious
Almost father-like
And kind
And he said why
Why apologize
What makes you think I need your sympathy
When today has been a **good** day
How do your eyes look at me as in need
When my happiness makes you question your happy
And why are you happy
Is what that man asked
With his pupils beaming through my exterior shell
Of clean clothes
And over-priced cologne
Only focusing on me
Just me
Not my appearance
And I stood speechless
Blank as a masterpiece
Once perfected but was erased
I felt deleted
He then reached into his pocket
His smile now more radiant than ever
And he handed me a piece paper
Himself holding it with two hands
As if this was his most prized treasure
And he said
Please
Read it
With his eyes brighter than the sunshine
On a North Carolina July
And he said it again
Please
Read it
That earth shattering voice now shaky
As if his interior was quaking

And beginning to break down
So I took the paper
Unfolding this man's trophy so delicately
Only using my index and thumb
The more I unfolded
The more spilled-out crumbs would empty from his importance
And I read this tarnished
Torn
And damn near worn out article
Titled "Hero"
Dated August 14, 2008
It explained a story of a man
Who was homeless
Down to his last
A man that slept on a bench in a park
Only fed by those who felt sorry
And wanted to help
And that man felt so sorry
That he couldn't even look at himself
So he tried
He tried to die
Jumped from a bridge in that park
One rainy day in that home of a park
And he fell
Broke leg
Bumped head
And body bled
The attempt at death failed
And he cried
As he cried he heard crying
As if his tears had an echo
And he found a child left alone
A child worried
Scared
And he yelled to that child come here
Help me and I shall help you
As I continued to read
Tears ran down that man's
That hero's face
As if his eyelids were replaced with storm clouds
And the clearing of the storm
Brought forth the smile of rainbow to be born
And he told me
Today was his 6-year Hero Anniversary
And he saved a life
Despite his sight and sometimes

Food-deprived nights
He was a hero and he looked at me
His eyes staring at my person
Looking at me
Making me look at me as worthless
This self-engaged materialistic manner of a person
And he asked me
What my worth is
And he reminded me
With that smile on his face
Like a kid in a race
Winning and being rewarded
With that medal of first place
That he was a hero
And he asked
Young man
What are you

Band Aids

My grandmother has told me before
That
Band Aids don't work for black people
She said that the severity of our scars
Are too deep
Wounds of unpaid wages
And permanent scraps
From past
Cracked whips
Make our skin heal faster
So
She never bought Band Aids
"Rinse it off and put a little dirt on it"
Is what she would say
I remember imagining
That the mixture
Of water
Dirt
And blood
Would act as mask
Covering up truth
Forcing my ancestors
Our ancestors
To wear lies
Layers of
How we were viewed
I can remember
Imagining the person
But
I could never imagine the pain
That expression of strength
The face of adversity
Sorrow-like
A soldier watching his best friend die
A piece in him dies
But he fights
Himself hit
By flying whip
But he stands
And puts a little dirt on it
I couldn't imagine
Imagine being forced to that mentality
Myself
Being a man who's quick

To put Band Aid on me
Over glimpses of blood
Makes me question my strength
And have I
Ever seen strength
Only seen take
Not what it takes
To just rinse off
And cover up
Mask
And act as wounds
Don't exist
Hidden in plain sight
Like the worries of the day
That people
Quite often throw a little dirt on
Or just rinse away
My grandmother tells me
She tells me
My generation
This plain sight wound
Of self-abuse
And hatred
Lack of patience
Is a damn shame
We just rely on Band Aids
Is what she says
Accountability
Null and void
And so quick to scream we hurt
If we only knew
My grandmother says
If we only knew that we healed faster
And that those Band Aids
They don't stick
Adhesive not built for our skin
So when I call her about my worries
Pains
And wounds
My grandmother tells me
To hold my head high
Fight through my pain
And just put a little damn dirt on it
I promise William
It will go away

Haiku
Music

Ears tainted by lies
Of glorified pied pipers
Turn off that music

Because it Seems

Extinction
An adjective meaning
No longer of any use or obsolete
Something dead or dying
Because the world views it as unnecessary
While at one time
The something was really here for a reason
The something had purpose
Worth and value
I wonder
I wonder sometimes if we are becoming
Or maybe have even become
Extinct
Or maybe not the "we"
Just the "it"
And by the "it"
I mean the awareness of our importance
The relevance of common sense
And a purpose of our person
While knowing our value
Because it seems
Because it seems
That the legacy
Of our existence
Has been tainted by
Ignorance
Intolerance
Misconceptions
And
Indifference
Not to mention
Our previous
Disposition
In a world
That reminds us
Every day
That we're unworthy
How do we reverse
What's been the norm
For so long
How do we break
The cycle

And overcome all the wrong
Because it seems
Because it seems
With a Martin Luther King Street in every city
A study showed more than 730 just in 2013
That the dream of that profound speech
Is just pacified with paved streets
And concrete illusions
Of what he wanted us to be
Which was more
He
Wanted
More
More than just
Accepting
We continue to fuel
The disrespecting
Of a place in this life
He stood for more
Dared more
To stand more
So I ask
Where are your feet
Because
The stand of a man
In this one-sided
Rude
And corruption of a land
Less are more apt
Maybe even scared to raise hands
For a purpose and reason
I've heard that change comes and goes with the seasons
So maybe
I wonder
And am even scared that
The relevance of global warming
And the change of our weather pattern
May just be that warning
That our chance for change has gone
Because it seems
Because it seems
We've lost sight
Of our ancestors
Insight
Lost in the dark
Unable to see

Light
Misdirected
Unable to
Think right
While activists are
Acting like activism
Is a peace fight
It just doesn't seem right
By any means necessary
Mentality
Is what we need
Fight
Against the misconception
And biased opinion
On the lips and pens
Of those that benefit from
Our oppression
Please believe
That's
The only way we'll reach
Our greatest potential
It's quintessential
To life
Because we know
They'll make anything we do
Good or bad
NEGATIVE
Because it ain't white
And that's
What the world is
Constantly seeing
And it ain't right
Listen to X's insight
"You don't have to be a man to fight
For freedom.
All you have to do
Is be an intelligent human being."
Think like Malcolm
eXemplify
Nothing but
Black greatness
We must
Overcome black hatred
Even if they
Continue to perpetuate it

I must repeat
We must overcome black hatred
Even if they
Continue to perpetuate it
Praise it
Celebrate it
And make it seem as if
We are the ones that created it
No need to negotiate
Or debate with it
Our current state of thinking is outdated
We must unite
Build nations and
Get educated
We are not
Slaves to this
Modern day
Glorification of nothing that makes sense
Hence the importance of these words spoken
The relevance of our minds being open
And the desire for change
And I'm hoping
Wishing and praying
That we are not just hoping
Wishing and praying
We need more
To stand more
I dare more
To change
Because it seems
That we have lost our want for anything
Complacent with the speech of dreams
We were supposed to be kings and queens
And seem to be lost in these streets
So I ask
So I ask
SO WE ASK
WHERE
ARE YOUR FEET

Kyd Kane and Endlesswill

Canvas

How are we supposed to change the image when the canvas is
Already painted before we even admire the beauty
We fuck before we've dated
And know this gift we have to offer one another has been tainted
But again that's just the canvas that is painted
Painted by society in so many different varieties
Growing up we see so such infidelity that blind eyes can see
Television shows with single parents
Endless stories of failed marriages
So many that who would even know where to start
I'm just saying that it seems inevitable that we all
Have broken or have had a broken heart
So truly can we view that relationship canvas as a work of art
Or just a picture that is viewed past along and used
Thrown to the back and abused
And is just looked at when we get that urge of loneliness
Then tossed away when that canvas gets annoying to us
Because everybody knows we can always get another picture
But ain't it crazy how those Mona Lisa's, Picasso's,
And Van Gogh's stick with us
Branded into our memory banks
There so we can appreciate a well-cared for canvas
And simply glance at the fake
But even forgery is desired as the effort of duplication is admired
And still hung in a frame but my question is that if that
Masterpiece isn't real isn't it just a game
An art gallery of facades, pretends or merely fakes
And considering this world's view on relationship
I question if we as artists can originally paint
Look at that tarnished, broken neglected canvas and see
Something great calmly using precise brush strokes because this
Should be your escape your getaway from the restraints but we
Only know what we are taught so eventually our time and efforts
Go to Waste we look at that canvas we created
And throw it away because the colors are not as vibrant
But believe me I have seen amazing shades of gray
So I refuse to never not paint
I will portray that perception of more than just affection
And hold onto my canvas until it is wanted not neglected
Treasured and protected
So I've got a priceless painting for sale
And I'm looking for an art gallery
Do you have any suggestions

Change Gonna Come

(After listening to the Sam Cook)
You see that's one of my favorite songs
And I really try to believe those words
In this world that depends on the poor
Pampers the rich and is so full of shit
It seems like our diaper is full
Full of defecation and piss
Excuse me I mean
Aggravation of the people pissed off
At those that are not potty trained
Excuse me again
I mean properly trained
But yet they make and enforce the decisions
Poisoning the passion of those pursuing better
As laws mimic viruses slowly eating up our insides
And want for change
Until our brains are sustained into this complacent lane
For example
No Child Left Behind
Like my son at 8
Gets all A's
Is an outstanding student
Isn't it prudent that that that should be acknowledged
However a child on his left a student who gets F's
Never tries his best
But passes to the next grade
I wonder where that really leaves the line
So therefore my son's effort for better
Is what is really left behind
Unknowingly forced to dumb down
Considering the downplay of the difference of desire
One failing
Mine excelling
But both get pushed on to the next phase
And he is aware
So he asks
"Dad, is it even worth it?"
Feeling his efforts are worthless
So I tell him
Shine
Reminding him that he is a star
And yes
There are more of you in the sky
But you

You shine bright
I tell him
My son
That he is the sun
Important in every angle of his life
Giving life and warmth
Heating up everything in his presence
Mine
And everyone's blessing
Without you
My world would be cold
So Josiah
Yes
It is worth it
Is what I tell my son
Effort is never worthless
And sadly seldom rewarded
However you should always do your best
I remind him that a bird picks sticks
And uses mud to build its home
Often doing it alone
Until it has a mansion of a nest
Singing songs in his haven
As the bird appreciates its sweat
And sometimes may have wanted to give up
But knew he needed a place to rest
I tell him
My son
Each pencil on paper
Each book read
And every problem solved are your sticks
And the annoyances of others are your mud
So son build
Construct your conscience
For your mental mansion
One day you will rest on your efforts
And then fly
Changing the outlook as I
Your father
Have tried and will continue to try
To change this view of effort
Change Gonna Come
My son
Oh yes it will...

Cloud 9

The bad thing about good yesterday's
Is that you miss them
Yesterday I literally laughed so hard
That my voice left me
Traveled to that place of forgotten
To reserve a seat for that moment that made me smile
Today I am sad
Because I know it won't return
So I am forced to remember
Retract
And recall that perfection
The seconds that seemed like hours
Of amazing
As if I was flying
Soaring through wonders of
Life
Peace
And
So much enjoyment in me
The bad thing about good yesterday's
Is that
They are often just a tease
Or glimpse
Of that once
Wanted to be repeated
Dream

Free

How far can you drive
Everyone says their dexterity
Can be compared to the
Expectancy of a sunrise
But what
Happens on longs nights
When the clockwork
Seems to make the clock not work
That tic-toc
Of being boxed
Living in the corner
Taking shots
From the obvious boss
That man that taunts
To show that he is "better"
As he boasts about his higher ranking
And the building of his stats
And he expects you to be thankful
To have feet on his mat
Putting on a show for
His land
His fans
To build his brand
And as an underdog
It's downright dumb to even think of an advance
So most of us workers
I mean contenders
Play pretender
Like we are just thankful for the house prize
Second place
Or in our place
Always knowing our position
As victim
Or worker bee
But what happens
When you want to fly free

Haiku
Running

Running for my life
Chased fast by failure's minions
Success please save me

Creative

My lungs are the ocean
Each breath taken opens the chance
For new creations to be found
Every exhale of air
Bring forth treasures buried in the depths of my body
That I didn't even know existed or maybe have just forgotten
I can't be silenced
My voice is broken alarm I promise I will be heard
Vocal cords replicating a storm cloud's constant flow
My movement is forever
I have endured so much pain
I've been burnt by the sun while being bullied by the rain
And I embrace the confrontation
Forced to accept that the wind controls my ways
I am pushed by blows of God's breath on my body
Like a toy boat on lake's surface
I am shaken by His thunder
But under he keeps me steady
Calm
Calm like a newborn in the arms of its mother for the first time
I'm protected
Protected like skin being contraceptive
Passion being erection and I penetrate mindset
Not worried of hate's infection
I am here for pleasure, comfort and amusement
Pillow talk being voice through lips
As they flow freely confident like the Mississippi
Eroding obstacles in my way by merely existing
While I more than just exist
I fight
Fight like infant too ready for Earth's light
Climbed from womb early and labeled as preemie
The life is in me but I struggle
Poems being recitation
Audience incubation
Born but death being warned
But threat not stronger than the anticipation of my greatness
Because someone believes in me
Before I was aware they said that they needed me
So I fight
I survive, I live, I write and I share
I am creative

I Am This

I am this
This meaning so much more than that
Of which what the world shows me as an it
Just a tool a hammer banging making noises
Building its buildings
Head aching and tarnished with each hit
But when the structure is done
My work being done
I have no place in it
Just another tool that's put away in a box
Until needed again
That's not me and it will never be me
I am no poster
Not a figure wearing chains that hang from neck
Forcing my head to drape just as low as those pendants
Filled with jewels
Diamonds and gold
I am my gold
My goal is to take it back
Rewind my story to those stories
Told before me of hands given for help
A story teller of triumph
Not David or Goliath
I am that rock
Thrown with full force launched out of sling
Hurled at the world making impact
I'm making my impact with this being
Me being there
Present
Showing an example
Leading by example
Expressing to my herd to never to digress on your words
Stay on topic and be heard
Teaching them that the world may not pick you first
But you will always be Daddy's top pick
I am reliable
Going against most pictures painted of my generation
Of mediocre rappers
Actors
Gangbangers
Thugs
Rhyming about shining
Money and drugs
A people bragging of nothing but self

A plague of people
Growing up wondering where their daddy was
I am that but I'm not raising this
I am
Repellent to oppression and self-hatred
Exude attitude and aggression
I'm raising happy
My care being water on flower love being sunlight for power
And it's beautiful
A beautiful strength
Strong like the back of Jesus carrying the burden of our lives
Beautiful like His eyes crying tears for our lives
Each footstep taken worth it and has purpose
I am his ankles
Strangled by the weight that has been placed on my back
Yet I still stand
Walking
Moving forward
I am the thank you
Appreciation to those who have led shown paths and bleed
Trickles of life showing a way for a better life
And I follow while leading
Taking charge
Like NBA center being rushed by guard
Grounded in my place
Ready for impact
I know this hit taken will not be for granted
So I stand
Planted
Roots spreading making the smooth
Surface of a facade rougher with my growth
I am that growth
Nourished by the doubt of those
Doubters who don't do and say that I couldn't
Because they didn't
Could have but wouldn't
So say that I shouldn't
I don't listen
My mind deaf to negativity because I know that if I listen
That will deaden the positive view in me
So to those of you who want better
Have promised self to never settle
Fallen but told themselves to get up
I am also you

If

If I were to get stopped by the cops
And happened to be a victim of racial profiling
And wound up getting shot
Dead right on the spot
I wonder
How would you remember me
And if a video surfaced of me cursing
At this authoritative person
Would you then say
That I got
What was meant for me
Therefore questioning my dignity
Even if you found out that my aggression
Was my only means for protection
But the officer still drew his weapon
Pulling trigger
Used terms like nigger
And made bullets penetrate
My head
Chest
And midsection
Would you
Then begin
To grieve for me
Would that grief mean helping my family
A hug for my mother
And a soothing conversation with my granny
Would you tell my kids
That their dad loved them with all of his heart
And that I had so much more life to live
And didn't deserve to die like this
Or
Would my departure provoke acts of violence
Riots
Protests
And aggression being misguided
Rage building like a caged lion
So the world roars
Roam streets
And communities are torn
I've heard
That life has to balance
So maybe it's a reasonable reaction
That the results of my death

Brings forth anger to be born
But then I wonder
Does violence stop violence
My driving
Ends with me being permanently silenced
My kids forever crying
So the world feels it must revenge
Triumph
Be rock in the controversy
Of David vs. Goliath
Am I
The one that bled
Life taken away suddenly unprepared for
Like breaths stolen away from a fish
Taken out of its environment
Why I gasp I must ask
Am I
Really being mourned
It seems to me
That if I am not able to live for me
That those who are still here
Will live for what I lived for
Creativity
Happiness
Being an example
And
The dismissal of negativity
Not Molotov cocktails thrown in the atmosphere
Or my brethren
And sisters
Getting thrown in jail
I don't understand
How the death of a man
Has an outcome of us destroying land
Giving the appointed authority
The want to have pistols pointed at me
Guns pointed at our faces
As if the black that we have been blessed with
Has a trace of bullseye
Going in headfirst
Is the worst
What happened to the appreciation of strategy
We cannot win like this

Lie

What if you were held accountable for each lie in life
Like each lie took away life from your favorite person
Each fib deteriorating rib
Words acting as sickle cell
Chopping away from your loved ones' insides
All because of lies as you watched knowing of the result
Would you stop literally put brakes on breath
Apply seatbelt to syllable and speak safe
Following the rules of the road
Paying attention to the signs as you spoke
Because you knew the drunk driving of a lie
Could result in the death of your favorite
Would you pay attention or not care
Because you were not be the victim
So you speak full speed
Baby not buckled in car seat
As you take shots of liquor
Swerving with your wording not caring and crash
You're fine
However
Where's your favorite
Truth could have saved them
Truth can save them
Have you ever noticed
What getting caught in a lie does to you
A part of you mourns what was and the once was
Will never be
The person on receiving end
Doubts more and more when you speak
Death of a relationship
Each lie spreading
Separating you from them
Puddle becomes ocean and you float on boat drifting away
Trying to dive to save life
But the lies or waves of your ways make it difficult to swim
They drowned from the lying habit
Truth was life jacket but they drowned
Pulled down by doubt
Your words became anchor on ankle so they sink
Belief in you weak
Now my question is
Do you care

Men Don't Cry

Men don't cry
We let our tears get drowned out in bottles of sorrow
Break down our heartache with our fingertips and let our downs get high
Where emotions are trapped in a short-term relax
Caged inside of the jail cell of an L
Bars being bars
And we are fed that three-course meal of forget in a glass
Where alcohol awakens the cure of amnesia so we can remember to just get over it
Forget or just force in and chain
Lock any emotions away that show any glimpse of strain
We can't break is what we say
But every cage has a gate so the short-term satisfaction doesn't last
I was told men don't cry
Our tear ducts are empty or maybe just replaced with hard luck
So when the pain of internal rain starts to take over our brain
We use phrases like
Fuck
I just need a minute
Or we sit in silence where our thoughts are typically clouded
Misguided from maintain to the course of actions of violence
Shouting provoked by enraged filled volcanic eruptions
Molten lava of madness burns away any rationalization in brain
Focus inflamed and when anything needs to be calmed
We wait on the calm of the rain
But when thoughts are clouded and clogged by unconscious
Decisions driven by hard times
How can sustain be drained
We men we can't cry
I don't cry
So my pen to does it for me
I transfer irritation to ink make my words sharp as a guillotine
And I stab paper with soliloquies
Cadence making cuts until each line bleeds
Stage being Band Aid
And I anticipate my healing because I'm hurting
But I've been told to hold it in
That as a man I can't let a tear shed
As if me masking my misfortune makes me more masculine
Men don't cry but most of the time
We want to

Content Capitalism

Can I talk to this country's conscience
Content
The constant violence and the abundance of death
As if there is an unbeknownst body count contest
A much needed conversation
On the separation of races
Our acceptance of segregation
And the willing but unwanted reliance for wealth
Or let's just talk about being mis-educated
Our knowledge being provided by the nation
Whose ulterior motives is their power being in control
And the reminder of us as a people
Staying in our strings' attached role by enforcing its fear
The ultimate puppeteer just demanding its rules
Of move when told move and prisons and stories told
By rebel corpses force us to just believe
In this perfect system that's teaching us follow
While destruction takes lead
It's sad how our vision seems to be so incomplete
We are all perfect leaves burdened by broken trees
Dreams being our shedding but our un-forgetting
Allows advance to blow in the breeze
Under these laws of corruption nothing is changing
Just more clouds of gunshots and the raining of bomb drops
And the re-programming of our brain
So many questions without answers as we wait for a better
When will we realize that we are the change
And we use words like hope to replace our efforts
Oh Miss America
The mother of our nation
We are breastfed your broken bread of hatred
While our imagination invents complacent creations
And the glorification of nothing
You life giver of lies and the appreciation of bluffing
Oh Miss America
I hate this picture that you repeat
Canvas being bloodshed on an easel of deceit
Paint brushes of mislead
Painters passion filled with greed
Oh Miss America
Why do you enjoy
Watching your land bleed?

Ghost

I died once
Maybe even more than once
But I really only can remember the last time
My thoughts and dreams being gagged by reality
Stabbed by unstable strides and were buried
Knife stuck in inconsistency's chest
Penetrating my last breath
Like a hole in the tire
Of a car racing on the road to success
But detoured
To the cemetery of concrete expectations
My headstone reading
He wanted so much more
So here I stand just a ghost of the man
That failed
Spirit living to continue what my flesh
Only tried to do
It made attempts at purpose
But couldn't handle the burden of it not working
So it gave up
Jumped from tallest hope
Potential being rope
And choked
On foresight
Dreams dangling
Like the last leaf before winter
Absolutely having no chance of survival
But it tried
Is what I'm forced to remember
As if trying is good enough
But I know trying
Doesn't do a damn thing
Only reminds me of not winning
Recalls missing
And brings forth the memories of not being good enough
So I continue
As the ghost of misfortune's past
And a better man's future
Present state feeding on potential will
I'm haunted by the hunger
Of what could've
Horrified by what didn't
So continuing is my commitment
This soul has a purpose

Person was worthless
Unable to handle the hardships
So self-sank to the bottom
Of opportunity's ocean
Drowning by the waters of what
Should have become
And the deeper I sink
The pressure makes me think
That while I was alive
I was just weak
So this spirit
Takes the place for what will be
A better man
Stronger
And with these new ghostly powers
Walls don't even make sense
I walk through them
Continuing to move forward
Nothing can stop me now
I laugh at blockades' challenge
Ignoring the push of doubt
Trying to knock me off balance
Because ghosts don't worry
They just don't
I now have the ability to make others
Uneasy
With just my existence
While others don't believe what
They witness
As they are forced to remember
That for one to die and survive
Is just a lie
But that doubt only feeds my stride
Powers my prize
Of conquering this life
With my wants
I am now just a ghost
But those woes
Are my lows
That has made me
This ghost
Dead to doubt
But the funny thing is that
I'm better this way

Now

Is it bad that I still brag of you
I show people pictures of our life
As if it's still lived
Holding up your trophy
And I didn't even win
It has never been easy for me
To admit that I lost
Missed shot
And to pacify my pride
I blame it on distraction
Instead of lack of focus
As if there is a damn difference
I realize now
Realize that it was due to my
Lack of practice
Lack of patience
And
"For-self" mindset
I should have thought of you more
I wish on star
Almost every night
That I could take it back
Take all back
And do it now
I know
I know how to do it now
While I realize
That it's just
Too late to prove it

Officer Davis

She tells me
No, she demands that I to call her "Officer Davis"
She tells me and has told me for the last two years
That she wants to be a police officer and when I ask her why
Her reply is
"The world needs saving"
And she is very aware that the Batman's
The Wonder Woman's
And speed of light flight of the man in blue tights is not real
So she says she will be a real hero
That she is going to protect people
And I'm scared because I know my daughter will
Her will is that of me multiplied by 103
My daughter at the age of 7 is so brave and strong
Out of my kids she is the one I rarely see cry
She always goes to her room every time she is upset and hurt
I asked her why once and she told me
With her head held high that she leaves
Because when she is sad
When she is hurt and angry that is her time
Her strength is amazing
I remember one time my 9-year-old son
And 5-year-old son almost got into a fight
Not sure over what but before I could even speak up
She, my daughter asked them why
Before they could even give her a reply
She reminded them that they loved each other
And to play nice
They listened without any friction
They just listened
My daughter at 7 is a leader
I'm so happy to have her
Honestly I need her
So I'm scared of her passion her need for protecting
Because the relevance of the disrespecting
And fuck-the-police statements
How they are viewed as the one profession
That is the poster child for hatred
And the trending videos of them beating
Tazing and sending innocent lives to the grave
I'm not sure how my daughter
Little Miss Officer Davis
Is going to fit into that system

Preach

The teenagers in my neighborhood
They call me preach
And the smallest one
Out of the bunch
Told me that I
Talk
Too
Damn
Much
I laughed at his little disrespectful ass
And just
Kept
On
Talking
Preaching
From what they call it
But really
I just care
I care about their lungs
Considering
That our first real conversation was
"Do you know where I can get
Any smoke from bruhh"
Of course I said no
Followed by
"Why do you even smoke"
Their response was
"Why you don't"
As if I was missing out on
This amazing thing of being high
I'm too grounded by my preaching
Is what they say
I then explained
Told them of my change
Told them when I was their age
I did that
Sold packs
Sacks
Smoked everyday
Bagged up
Nicks
Zips
Q. P.'s
I was the man

That boy
Who could literally get anything
That those chasing a high would need
But
I woke up
Was a victim of life's
Sucker punch
Uppercut
Kick to the gut
Beat the fuck up
For drugs
Money and
That life
At this point of the conversation
Those teens
My congregation
Was into my preaching
I had captured their attention
Had their adolescent minds
Attracted by my crimes
So that's when I mentioned
That now
I spend many nights wishing
That someone
Anyone
Would have talked to me
And my previous statement
Of me being beat
Should not be taken literally
But mentally I'm scared
Internally bleeding
And
Thoughts clouded
From my baggage
I told them that
In high school I graduated
With a 3.6 grade point average
But was blinded
By my bagging
So I stopped trying to get smarter
I told them that after
I graduated I went to college
I was going to play ball
Went to a couple practices and all
Had people in awe

I was going to be a starter
But blunts I sparked up
Made my lung capacity smaller
So that inhaling
Lead to me failing
Had so much talent
But didn't know how to balance
And my adolescent arrogant ass
Didn't care
I was too fly
With new the gear
Had the ladies in my ear
So unaware to the real
So I stopped trying
For money
For that thrill
Drive killed for better
From lack of guidance
At this point of my preaching
They stood in silence
And were hooked onto every word
So I continued
Continued to speak
Preach
Is what they call it
I told them
That y'all are helping
Helping the world keep y'all weak
Why don't y'all see
The world sees y'all young assess
Standing on this street
Pants down
Damn near to your feet
What do you think
The world thinks
They think you're nothing
And y'all are helping
Helping how we are viewed by police
Have you not seen the latest trend
And I am not talking
About Versace
Designer jeans
Polo clothes
Or the Jays y'all are in
I'm referring to the law
Making people comfortable

To be uncomfortable
With the color of our skin
As if there is a virus
Or plague
By the name of melanin
Are y'all listening
Because I care
And have been there
So I am asking
Preaching
Hand outreaching
Letting you know I'm there
And if you need someone to talk to
Call me

Save Me

God please save me
I am just a fingertip grip on the edge and I don't know
How much more this ledge can take of me
I really fear that failure's near
There is so much that I've made it through
I've been stressed
Depressed and anger filled emotions
Have put this chemical imbalance inside of my chest
A mixture compiled with Christ and worry of this life
And I'm sorry God because life is winning
Because I'm losing
Myself
Lost in my losing
And it hurts
I've been working 24/7
Appreciating my blessings towards right
But it seems it just won't work
And I've been told
Many a time
Repeatedly
As if phrases are fight songs
By those who have felt the need to teach
That
God
Is what they would say
God won't give you more than you can bear and that
My feet still stand so I better keep going
But these burdens of worry are like a bear
Attacking its prey and I'm starting to worry
Of what does that make me
The one eating or the weak
So I drop to my knees
And I pray
And beg
Help me Lord
Protect my world from this global warming of worry
Save me from the severities
Of my despair
God I'm asking
Crying
God I'm
Begging
For your help

Smile

If you could imagine an angel
A lady angel
God's favorite angel
Eating her favorite fruit
While reading her favorite book on her birthday
Just a day filled with joy
Now close your eyes and imagine that angel's face
That expression of happiness
Literally the best smile an angel can give
Magnify that joyfulness by 10 and you'd have my mother's smile
A smile so real and big that's what everyone usually notices first
An introduction with dimple on cheek, squinted eyes
Teeth brighter than a full moon on a cloudless summer night
You really can't help but notice and even smile back
I remember when I was a kid
My mom and I would play this game
It didn't have a name and really didn't even make much sense
I would make silly voices mimicking her favorite cartoons
And I would win when she laughed I would always win
That's one of my favorite past memories
I have put it away in life's case locked safe
And glance when I need to smile
Her smile is what you gave me
A smile
Hand drawn by God
On paper made from trees
That grew in his garden
He etched each intricacy
Putting so much detail into a smile
That I have no choice but to believe in him
And his want for my happiness
Because as I was born
And opened eyes for first time
Her smile is what I seen
Enhanced by bright hospital light
I saw God in the gleam
They say
I have heard that when I was born I didn't cry
I'm 100% sure
That my mother's smile is the reason why
I love you mom

Edge of the Bed and Love

Stuck between the edge of the bed and love
On one side
I'm inches away from inception
Activities of life and the determination of busy
The constant of chaos
Work
Entertain
Parent
Be apparent
Notice
Focus
Don't fail
Stand up
Hold hand
And
No, you can't have a piece of candy before breakfast
Kind of day
And on the other
The flip side to worker bee on caffeine
Is quiet
Serene and soft
Soothing
Like a bubble bath on a tense body
Calm like the first kiss after a long night's sleep
In the arms of perfection
Your lips still taste like the dream
Where we first met in a crowded place
That was comforted by the foresight of forever
I am lucky enough to sleep next to love
Pillow being person
Hand-picked by Cupid
While he wove this blanket of
Thankfulness
With the sharpest most reliable arrow in his case
Our bed
Wherever we make rest knowing that any place is Home
When relaxation is accompanied by hope
That is always fulfilled with a new day
I lay next to love each night
While being awakened with my arms overflowing with my future
Of knowing that forever
My nights will be the same

I Love you Cathey

Super Hero

Look up in the sky it's a bird
No, it's a plane
No, it's a father playing games
Jumping from swings being there for his kids
Fully equipped with a backpack
Full of juice boxes and fruit snacks
Tennis shoes so he can run fast
And a smile that represents his life
An ear-to-ear grin that works every facial muscle within
His impenetrable parent-powered skin
That he uses for late night book reading
Silly kisses
And the comforting look during the goodnight tuck-ins
He is
I am a hero
My mission
One that I refuse to neglect
Is to protect, respect, and deflect any doubt
Spoken from my children's mouths
Like my melanin was made of elastic
Trampling the self-defeating thoughts
That are brought
From the lack thereof materials that are bought
I am showing that nothing is greater
No money or diamond
Nor celebrity
Can triumph over a heart that is growing
Or manipulate a mind that is knowing
So learn
Is what I chant to my little justice league of future good-deed-
doers
Again I am a hero
Their leader
Leading by example
Preaching do as I say
And I know that that my little minions have inherited my keen
vision
So I know that they will do as I do
So I try
Wings spread ready to fly
Doubt being the villain
It's shooting its pistol of pessimism in my direction
But my foresight for better days
Help power my defense mechanism

So I am shielded from the sadness of excuses
Worry is useless when I have the melody
"My minions' laughter" as my theme music
I am Super Dad
That's what they call me
That's proof that even if Marvel and DC combined
Made a man with the power of Superman
The utility belt of Batman
Hulk's strength
Spiderman's agility
And Flash's speed multiplied by 3
Still wouldn't have enough energy to compare
To the father that you see
This back has the strength of 100 men
I've done enough piggy back rides to walk across 10 lands
Colored enough with this hand
To fill a paper big enough to cover France
And the funny part is I just began
I am not going anywhere
So what you see here
This is just a disguise
I have revealed my secret identity to you
Cherish it with your life
What you see as a mere poet
This man will return to his responsibilities
Tonight
So I am just a poet for the moment
But a father for life
I stand for my sons and daughters
Them being here
Has been what powers my fight
And they are aware of my ability
So there acknowledgment of loving me
Gives me this eagle vision
For foresight
I am able
To look pass incapable
I
Am Super Dad

Tired

I'm tired
Tired like I have driven past my limit of tread
And need to change my tires
They are worn out from my travels
And I am afraid that I am one speed bump away from just
POPPING
I'm tired
Tired of being stranded
Stranded without a spare
No Triple A and my cell phone battery has just died so how can I
call for help
So I am left to wait with my damn hand out just expecting
Reluctant to ask and apprehensive to accept
So why should I expect
Thumb out hitchhiking my way through struggle
As I travel left in front of right shadowed by lies
And I walk on Main Street
Its intersection compromise
You will find me on the corner holding my sign
"Will do anything to provide"
Unfortunately that's what it feels like
Poster child of the working man
Dirty pants
Callused hands
2016 new century slave
I'm tired of slaving
Being a slave to the working class
Class is what they call it
I've been in it for only 10 years
Some stay in the this class for over 30+
The school of hard knocks being the university
But when will I get my grades
Graduate
Upgrade
I'm so tired of the same
Tired of the repetition
5:00 a. m. get up and work
6 p. m. get off work
Sleep
10:30 p. m. wake up
11 p. m. work
4:30 a. m. drive
5:00 a. m. sleep
7:00 a. m. work

Work
Work
I'm so........so tired
Tired of working 7 days a week and only having enough money
to survive for 5
So I'm forced to borrow funds to live on the other 2
A couple times a month I try to escape from being tired
So I use money to run away from being chased by hard times
But after the fun has gone and I'm forced back to the grind
Of being tired
Tired like I question what tired is like
When there isn't anything to be liked about being tired
It's just exhausting

Bruce Jenner

To Bruce Jenner,
I have a question for you
Nothing that is disrespectful I promise
It's almost like that are aliens even real question
There really isn't a right answer
And I'm not even sure if there is an answer
I'm just really curious if you love yourself now
And I don't mean now that you have switched
From firm handshake grip to French manicure tips
Or any of that other shit
That I personally me a proud
Born and bred to stand when I pee man
Don't understand
How you a man
A father would want to be woman
And again I am just curious
If you're actually happy now
Now that the world knows your business
Have fallen victim
Tripped over importance to notice
What
To notice nothing
We have paid attention to blank canvas and call it original
Amazing
As if we haven't seen this or are not seeing this daily
It drives me crazy
And I'm not hating on the Transgender
The gay
The woman on woman
It has nothing to do with me for what someone self seeks
I just don't understand the relevancy
The need to be on TV
On magazine
On Food Lion isle eye-level to a child
Is it so they can question
Because that's the impression
That is going to lead from your confession
Of the new you
By the name of Caitlyn
Can you please have
Her or You
Tell me why
We needed to know....

Too Much

I have come to the conclusion
Placed notary stamp on realization
Literally just stopped wondering why
And have accepted
That I think about you way too much
For some strange reason you come to mind for no reason
Like when I wake up and take my head off of the pillow
And thank God for the ability to do so
Something in me also has me thank him for you
And I smile
This makes me think of your smile
And now I'm happy
Not even 5 minutes into my day
While taking the time to pray
Mixed with recalling images of your face
And I'm happy
Ready to conquer the world
Fighting with hope in hand
And anticipation as my shield
Prepared to defend my joy
That's what you've done to me
All from
Just a kiss
A moment
That replays in my mind
Of a time when
My lips were stained from your perfection
I can still taste your smile
It reminds me of
An ocean breeze
Mixed with the warmth of the sun
And hint of strawberries
Those are all my are favorites
And when I kissed you
Those are the things I were able to taste
So relaxation is what your flavor is
I really do think about you too much
But if me thinking
Is my way of seeing you
Then I'm sure that I'm not thinking enough.

Twenty-Eight

3/11/1987
Is the day my name got on the list to get into heaven
After 28 years of lies and many failed tries
I'm sure that my name has been erased
More than once or twice
And with the scars from this life of war
I'm sure
That God can barely recognize my face
But fate
Has placed poetry onto my plate
So I season
Each sentence
Bake and then taste
Savor and escape
From a life of a never ending rat race
And I write
I read
And recite
And I get a lift
From God's gift
So after 28 years
I've made it here
Shed many tears
But nothing has been a waste
So even if don't receive a single present today
My presence today
Is more than enough
For all my heart and soul
To give sincere thanks

Heartless

I'm not heartless
I just only have a little heart left
So I use my heart less
My mind masking my heart's wants
Because my heart doesn't know what's best
My heart's past decisions
Have only brought stress
So my lack thereof of longing for love
Is there
Because the love that's left there
I'll die to protect

A Dream

A dream to me starts out as a seed
Planted or more or less implanted into your thoughts
This is then watered with accomplishments and more goals
And as it basks in the sun you see that it will begin to grow
So as you care for it the right way you can begin to approach
The need to give your dream everything it needs
To be reality
Instead of something you only think about when you're sleep
But relevant when you're awake
And transforms from a dream into fate
Caring for it in the right way
Giving it your all and everything that it takes
To flourish into something real
Instead of only relevant in a dream's state
Which leaves me ask
When will you awake

[Wrong]
Love

I feel love is like a beautiful dove
Because it is wonderful why it is here but you know that it will be gone
And it drives you to question the thought of why it was just a tease
For that minimal moment your heart was at ease
But that's false hope because you know that it will leave
Whether that love fades or it's deceased
And it's disappointing because since you've had love before
Your want for it has increased
And you wonder if without it can you truly have inner peace
So for me
Love is just a four letter word ending in "E"
That fuels emotions that result in stupidity
Humility
And finishes up at idiosyncrasy
It could be the lack of loyalty the reason why love is annoying to me
Or the fact that when it's described I'm jealous because that isn't the joy that I see
Arguably I've compared love to a tree and I portray the possibility of me being a leaf
Falling off the branch
Blowing in the breeze
Landing on the ground slowly diminishing
And it hurts
But the pain is like rain
So it helps for the replenishing

Memory

I must admit to you something
And please be hesitant to start judging
But I am scared of
ME
Fucking horrified of my possibilities
Because I know of what I have done
Thinking I am pursuing right
But setting myself up subconsciously to do wrong
So in reality is wrong what I really want
Or more so what I really wanted
I feel haunted by a ghost of this man's memories
And tormented by the skeletons in his closet
Unfortunately that's my closet
As I lay awake at night afraid of the lies rising up from the dead
Freeing themselves from the prison in head
And making themselves present in my present
Feeling threatened by my reflection and the secrets he may tell
As he laughs when we are eye to eye
Because despite that I stand with pride
There are things that I still hide and even though it may seem
That I have succeeded
Deep down I feel that I have failed
Internally defeated
Covered with the stench of dead
Dying dreams the exact smell
As the fumes forever follow me as a reminder
A remembrance of the times of my lack of commitment
Like
Sinning but yelling Christian
At one time being married and falling victim
To not playing my part
And being deceitful
Using these words as a flute
Charming snakes
Right out of their baskets
Then
Simply playing with their hearts
Using them simply as show pieces
Trophies on my mantle
Committing suicide without knowing it
Trying to pick apart relationships
When in the end my heart gets dismantled
Self-heart surgery
Ruining my wants

Literally standing in my own way
Running with shoes untied
Knowingly blocking the pursuit of my purpose
At times I have felt so damn worthless
Like I'm eyes closed searching
For something
Then when I feel as if I have found that something
I open my eyes and see nothing
All hopes let down
Living through the tears of a clown
Because even though you see me smile
Deep down I may have already drowned
From the tears that I didn't
Or couldn't let out
Internally flooded
From my attempts at victory
But fallen slightly short
Treated life as a game
Often hating to play
While being a fan of the sport
My own contradiction
My conscience feeling conflicted
Because I've fallen victim to dwelling on negative times
So my rights are restricted
Thoughts are twisted
Intertwined thinking torn between
What I have seen
And what I want to see
As I try my best to not let my yesterday truly define me
While preparing my present
For a positive future
Tomorrow treated as a gift
Awaited
Like a present under the Christmas tree
Or a child seeing a fallen star
And making the magical wish
Waking up the next day a seeing what he asked for
So my bad memories
I treat as mementos
Reminding me to grasp more
That's how I reflect
Or more so
Respect my past thoughts
How do reflect on yours

Relationship View

I wake up sometimes and I'm just horrified
Monster movies brought forth to reality in front of my eyes
All this danger glorified
When will we realize that we are our own demise
Dreams beat down to death
Living like Walking Dead
Seems feelings have fled
As we tend to feed on flesh
I admit I have even bitten on breast
Exposing arteries
To make it easier for the heart to be torn from chest
On the back of necks
Lungs let go of last breaths
A damn zombie
However
Before you judge my endeavors
Just know that also my heart has been taken from me
Ripped away from its safe
Put in front of my face
Held in her palm
As I watched my blood drip around arm
Taunting me with each blood splatter
Each drip echoes the harsh realization
That in this generation compiled around hatred
That love and everything deriving around that thought
Doesn't matter
So it's not my fault
We all have heard the phrase
"One only knows what they are taught"
So I refuse to apologize for being studious
And passing my classes with all A's
Valedictorian to dismay
Team captain to this game to play
Of Russian roulette
Loved passed around
Being shot done with harsh threats
As I wallow in my sorrow
I prepare for the opponent to face next
Covered in this rubber of protection
My weapon penetrates midsections
Shielded from the sins of society
However emotions are left as open targets
Picked off as if they are front line men

And I say so sincerely
That I cringe and something dies in me
Each time I start hearing that
"Sex and feelings do not correlate"
That
"Nowadays you can fuck without the date"
And
"Give them just enough
That they never have enough
However
Never give them all that it takes"
Because
"So often when one does
The one that seems to have did
Is more so left with the discouragement of heartache"
So what are the choices
To love
Or just love disappointment
Or can the disappointment be avoided
Two forming one
Seed to earth
Basking in love's birth
Shielded from society
In the shade of us surrounding
United in enjoyment
Yet
Too often feelings are toyed with
Taking time to build each block
Being passionate about the placement of each spot
Then as you finish to admire what you've got
You smile at the effort
You may even take a picture
But you always break it down
It's always seems so easy to let go

Tomorrow

I can't wait until my tomorrow
Because as I live today
Going about my way
Not really knowing the right things to do or say
I think about sorrow
And things I should have done
Places I should have gone
But didn't
A mere victim of my today
My present
My neglect
My self-disrespect
Of wrong choices
So I think about tomorrow and ways to avoid this
Disappointment of me
And positions I have put myself in the past
To face defeat
I want to ensure that it isn't on repeat
So I can ultimately succeed at life
Being able to fall and learn from it
To ensure the mistakes don't happen twice
And are able to encounter the same situation
But being able to handle it right
To be right
So as I awake and go about my day
I wait for the night
This is then followed
By my promises of tomorrow

Words of Wisdom (3)

I am finally rich
And will never again be poor
My wealth is in my happiness

What's yours

Proof

Straight from the root
I am the proof
Why one should never say what's the use
Or make an excuse
Follow groups
Because you have what it takes
For groups to follow you
With your voice
So each choice
Brings you closer
With each chance
To enhance
So I wake up every day telling myself
I am the man
While at the same time striving to be
My ULTIMATE MAN

This book is a dedication to poetry, family, friends, and will. William "Endlesswill" Davis contributes the upmost gratitude and appreciation given to all his contacts for listening, critiquing, and believing in his talents.

Without you all he would have never pursued his passion

-Thank you all-

Special Thanks to
Cathey Stanley, Dasan Ahanu, Church Da Poet,
John Lacabiere III, Patrice Ingram, Melissa Willis
Joe Howard, Jaysen King, Roxanne Sykes, Tena Haywood
Barbara Haywood, Tinne Mae Davis, Annie Summers
LeDarrius Turner, Von Green, William Davis Sr.
and poetry

William Davis Jr
Endlesswill

If you're inspired write your own
poems, notes, responses, short stories,
drawings, math problems, jokes,
anything just **#writeheavy**

Notes:

Notes:

Notes:

Notes: